Who is Jesus?

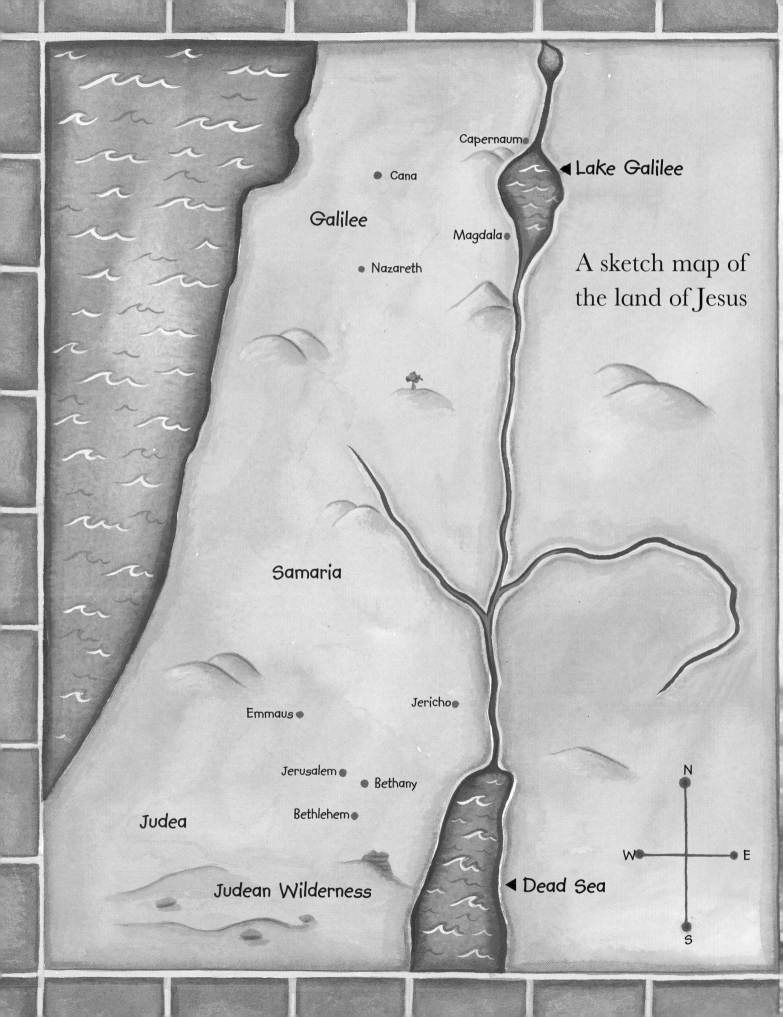

Capernaum

Cana

Galilee

Magdala

◄ Lake Galilee

Nazareth

A sketch map of
the land of Jesus

Samaria

Jericho

Emmaus

Jerusalem

Bethany

Bethlehem

Judea

N

Judean Wilderness

◄ Dead Sea

W   E

S

Who is Jesus?

Jesus is someone
who lived 2000 years
ago, in a land called
Palestine. The stories
about him say he
was special from
the beginning...

Sarah Hall

Illustrated by
Lisa Berkshire

LION
Children's Books

Published by
Lion Publishing plc
Sandy Lane West, Oxford, England
www.lion-publishing.co.uk
ISBN 0 7459 4298 9
Lion Publishing
4050 Lee Vance View, Colorado Springs,
CO 80918, USA
ISBN 0 7459 4298 9

First UK edition 2001
1 3 5 7 9 10 8 6 4 2 0
First US edition 2001
1 3 5 7 9 10 8 6 4 2 0

A catalogue record for this book is available
from the British Library

Library of Congress CIP data applied for

Typeset in 14/22 Baskerville MT Schlbk
Printed and bound in Singapore

Contents

1 A Message from an Angel

In a little hillside town called Nazareth lived a girl named Mary. One day an angel came to her. Mary was astonished. She was also a bit scared. 'Don't be afraid,' said the angel. 'God has chosen you to be special. You are going to have a baby. The child will be God's Son. You are to call him Jesus.'

Mary still didn't understand. 'How can I have a baby?' she asked. 'I'm not yet married.'

'God will make it all come true,' said the angel.

'I will do as God wants,' Mary replied.

 Mary was the mother of Jesus. When the angel came, she was living with her parents, helping to look after the home.

'There is more news,' said the angel. 'Your cousin Elizabeth is going to have a baby too, even though she is very old.'

Mary went to visit Elizabeth to talk about their news.

 Elizabeth was Mary's cousin. Here, she is talking to Mary on the flat roof of her house. Behind are tiny fields called terraces, cut into the hillside.

Jesus is Born

Now Mary was expecting her baby. An angel spoke to the man she had promised to marry: 'Joseph, take care of Mary and her baby.'

Joseph agreed. 'We will be a family,' he said to Mary. 'You know that the Romans who rule us want to count everyone. I have to go to Bethlehem to put my name on their list, because my family comes from there. Let's go together.'

So they did. The town was crowded. Mary and Joseph had to stay in a stable. There, Jesus was born.

That night, shepherds were out on the hills looking after their sheep. An angel appeared.

'Good news!' said the angel. 'A baby has been born. He is going to help people live the right way and make God's promise come true. You will find him lying in a manger.'

And so they did.

Mary and Joseph had to shelter in a stable. There, Mary's baby Jesus was born. For a cradle they used a manger – a trough for animal feed.

 The shepherds let their sheep graze during the day. At night they led them into a pen called a fold. As they guarded the doorway on the night Jesus was born, the shepherds saw angels.

3 Jesus and the Wise Men

At the time when Jesus was born, a bright star appeared in the sky. In far-off lands to the east, wise men saw it.

'This star tells us that a new king has been born,' they agreed.

They followed the star. It led them to Palestine. In the city of Jerusalem they asked if anyone knew about a new king.

The king in Jerusalem was Herod. He was angry – and scared – at the news. He asked *his* wise men for advice. Then he met the wise men from the east.

'People believe that a great king will be born in Bethlehem,' he said to the travellers. 'Go and find out where he is – then tell me.'

The wise men found Jesus. They gave rich gifts: gold, frankincense and myrrh. Then they set off for home, but they did not go back to Herod.

An angel spoke to Joseph: 'Hurry! King Herod has heard of your child. He wants to kill him. You must go to live in Egypt until it is safe to come back here.'

King Herod ruled the land of Palestine for the Romans. He had many people killed in his fight to be king, including his own wife. He was worried when he heard that a king had been born. Jesus and his family escaped, but Herod's soldiers killed many boy babies to try to get rid of Jesus.

An angel warned Joseph in a dream to escape from King Herod. He took his family to Egypt. They travelled for many days to get there.

4 Jesus Grows Up

When Joseph and Mary heard that Herod had died, they went back to Nazareth. There, Jesus grew up with the other children in the little town.

 Here, Jesus is playing a game.

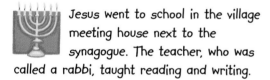 Jesus went to school in the village meeting house next to the synagogue. The teacher, who was called a rabbi, taught reading and writing.

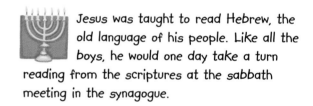 Jesus was taught to read Hebrew, the old language of his people. Like all the boys, he would one day take a turn reading from the scriptures at the sabbath meeting in the synagogue.

A boy would learn his father's trade. It is likely that Joseph taught Jesus how to be a carpenter.

5 Jesus in the Temple

When Jesus was twelve, he was old enough to go to the Temple in Jerusalem for the Passover festival. At Passover Jewish people celebrated how God once rescued them from slavery. He went with his family and a crowd of people from Nazareth.

At the end of the celebrations, everyone set off for home. In the evening Mary and Joseph found out that Jesus was not in the group.

They hurried back, feeling very worried. They looked high and low. At last they found Jesus. He was talking to wise teachers in the Temple. He was asking questions about God and giving good answers of his own.

'Why did you do this and make us worry?' asked Mary.

'This is my Father's house,' said Jesus, 'you shouldn't have worried about me. You should have known I'd be here.'

Jesus travelled to Jerusalem with a crowd from Nazareth. They saw the Temple in Jerusalem from far off. It was built on a hill.

Here, Jesus is sitting with the teachers in the colonnade of the Temple. The teachers had studied the ancient books of their people – their scriptures. They knew a lot about their history and their God.

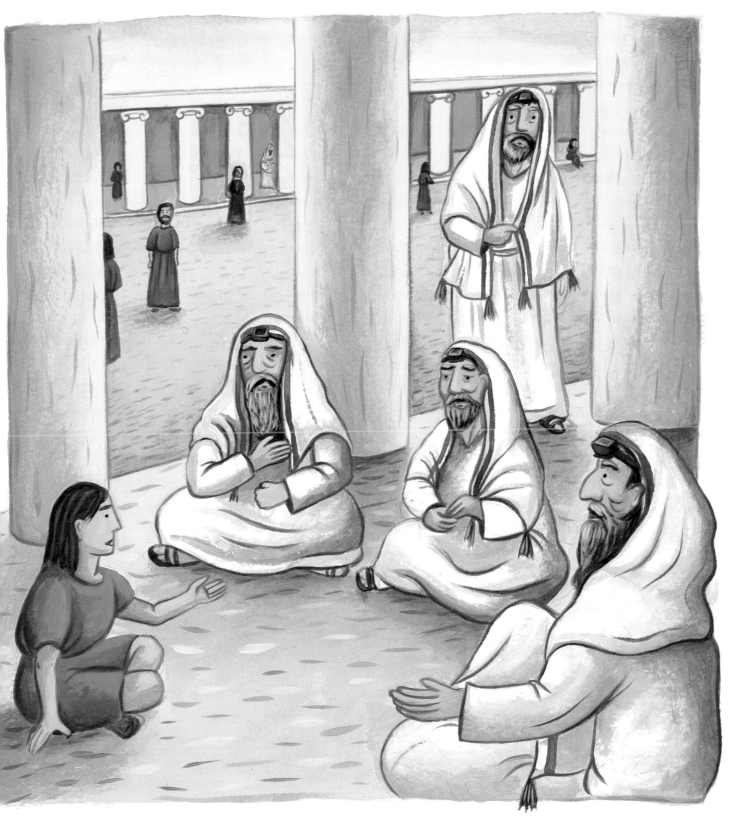

Jesus is Baptized

Mary watched her son Jesus grow up into a young man.

Mary's cousin Elizabeth also watched *her* son grow up. His name was John and he was a prophet: people believed he saw things as God sees them. He lived in the wild desert and people came to hear his wise words.

He told people to change their ways and live as God wanted. Some decided to make a new start. John baptized them – he washed them in the River Jordan as a sign of saying goodbye to their old ways and starting again.

Jesus' cousin John was a prophet. He wore rough clothes and had long hair and a beard. All kinds of people came to listen to what John had to say.

One day, John saw Jesus waiting in the crowd to be baptized. John knew that Jesus had done nothing wrong and that he didn't need to make a new start. But Jesus wanted to be treated in the same way as everyone else.

As Jesus came up out of the water, people saw a dove settle on him. It was the sign of God's Spirit. Jesus heard God's voice saying, 'You are my Son. I love you and I'm pleased with you.'

 Jesus was baptized by John in the River Jordan. From then on, Jesus began his work that changed the world.

7 Jesus in the Desert

Jesus left his ordinary work. He believed God told him to go into the wild desert to think about what to do next. The devil came to try to stop him. He waited until Jesus had not eaten for days and was very hungry.

'You could turn these stones into bread,' said the devil.

'No,' replied Jesus. 'The scriptures say that people need more than just bread – they need to listen to God too.'

'Do something clever and dangerous to show people you're special,' said the devil. 'God will look after you.'

'No,' replied Jesus. 'The scriptures say it is not right to test God.'

'If you do as I say, I'll make you king of all the world,' said the devil.

'No,' replied Jesus. 'The scriptures say that God is the only one to obey.'

Then the devil went away.

bear   jackal   lion

Jesus spent time in the desert.
He was all alone with God –
and the wild animals.

wolf

leopard

snake

8 Jesus and his Friends

Jesus set out to follow God's ways. He chose friends to help him. They were all very different. Two pairs of brothers were fishermen: Simon and Andrew, James and John. Simon's nickname was Peter, the rock. Philip was from Simon and Andrew's town. Matthew used to be a tax collector *for* the Romans; another Simon used to be a freedom fighter *against* the Romans. Then there was Thomas, another James, Thaddeus, Bartholomew and Judas.

Women and children were followers of Jesus too. Mary from the little town of Magdala was one of them.

They didn't have much time left for the jobs they used to do! Other friends of Jesus gave them places to stay and food to eat as they travelled around.

 Jesus chose all kinds of people to be his friends. He welcomed women and children who came to listen to him.

 Jesus' friend Matthew used to be a tax collector. Here, he holds scales for weighing coins.

 Jesus' friend Simon used to be a freedom fighter. He wanted to get rid of the Romans. Here, he holds a sword.

Some of Jesus' friends were fishermen on Lake Galilee. Here, Simon and Andrew hold one end of a fishing net in their boat. James and John hold the other end of the net in theirs. As the boats move, fish get caught in the net.

9 Jesus and the Wedding

One day, Jesus and his friends were invited to a big wedding. Then came a whisper of bad news: 'The wine has run out. How embarrassing!'

Jesus' mother turned to him. 'You must do something to help!' she said.

'It's not the right time for me to do anything,' said Jesus.

But his mother said to the waiters, 'Do whatever he tells you.'

Jesus told them to fill big stone jars with water. Then he told them to pour it out. It had turned into wine!

The person in charge of the party tasted it. 'This is the best wine of all,' he declared.

A wedding in Jesus' day. Here, the bridegroom is carried by his friends to meet his bride.

Here, the bride and groom are sitting under the wedding canopy, wearing their fine clothes.

Here, the guests dance and sing at the party.

10 Jesus and the Storm

Jesus travelled with his friends to the villages on both shores of Lake Galilee. His fishermen friends used to sail the boat that carried them. One dark night, a sudden storm blew up. The boat was tossed and battered.

'Help!' shouted the men. 'We're going to die.'

Jesus was asleep in the boat. 'Wake up!' they cried.

Jesus stood up.

'Hush,' he said to the wind. 'Be still,' he said to the waves. The storm went away at once. Jesus' friends were astonished.

'Who can Jesus be?' they wondered.

 The kind of fishing boat Jesus travelled in had a sail and a steering oar. It was only just big enough for Jesus and his friends.

11 Jesus and the Roman Soldier

People soon began to talk about Jesus. He could work wonders – miracles! He could even make sick people better with just a touch.

One day, a Roman officer's servant was sick. The officer hurried off to meet the miracle worker and pleaded for help, though he knew some Jews didn't like Romans.

'I will come,' said Jesus.

'Oh, I don't deserve that,' said the soldier. 'Just give the order. I give orders to people and they do as I want. If you give an order, that will be enough.'

Jesus was surprised. 'My own people don't trust me as much as this Roman does,' he said to the crowds. 'But all kinds of people can be friends with God. Now go home,' he said to the officer, 'and you will find that what you hope for will happen.'

The man went home. His servant was well.

 Here, a Roman soldier is talking to Jesus. He is wearing chain armour.

Jesus healed a Roman servant. Here, two servants take care of the house for a rich Roman couple.

Roman servants

a rich Roman couple

the rich man giving orders to his servants

12 Jesus and the Man Who Couldn't Walk

Four men sat and thought. Their friend was sick. He couldn't move. 'Jesus is in the house over there,' they muttered. 'But there are so many people crowding near we can't take our friend to see him.' Then they had a clever idea. 'Let's break through the roof above his head and lower our friend in his bed through the hole!' they said.

They walked up the steps to the flat roof. They made a hole in the roof and lowered their friend through it – down to Jesus.

Jesus smiled. 'Your friends have a lot of faith in me,' he said to the sick man. Then he added, 'Your sins are forgiven.'

The religious leaders were shocked. 'Only God can forgive people,' they whispered. 'Jesus isn't *allowed* to say that.'

Jesus knew what they were thinking. 'Is it easier to say, "Your sins are forgiven," or "Get up and walk"?' he asked. Then he said to the man, 'Get up and walk. Take your bed home.' And he did.

 Here, four men carry their sick friend onto the roof of the house. Most houses had an outdoor staircase to the roof. Roofs were used as a place to store things and to sleep on hot nights.

Here, four men make a hole in the roof to take their friend to Jesus. Houses in Palestine had flat roofs which needed to be mended regularly. It was quite easy to make a hole – and to repair it.

13 Jesus the Storyteller

People came in crowds to hear Jesus, because he told good stories. They seemed to be about everyday life, but they had a special meaning. They were about God and what it's like when people live God's way – in God's kingdom.

'Here's a story,' said Jesus one day at a party. 'The story is about a party. A rich man wanted to have a great feast. He invited his friends and they agreed to come. So he made his plans and sent a second message: "Come, everything's ready."

'"Oh dear," said the first. "I'm busy…"

'One by one, they all made excuses.

'The party-giver was angry. "Right," he said to his servant. "Go out and find people who will come… poor people, people who can't walk and who can't get jobs. They're not 'too busy'. They'll come."

'And they did… They hurried to the best party ever.'

 In Jesus' day, a party might be a feast. Here, people feast Roman-style, lying on couches around a low table to enjoy rich food.

grapes   figs   flat bread   wine

olives   vegetable soup   herb salad   roast meat

14 Stories About God's Kingdom

Jesus often spoke about 'the kingdom of heaven'.

'It is like a mustard seed,' Jesus said. 'You can hardly see it, but it grows into a tree big enough for birds to nest in.

'It is like yeast that you mix with flour to bake bread,' said Jesus. 'A tiny bit of yeast makes the dough rise to make good, soft bread.'

So what is the kingdom…? It is something small but it changes things in a big way.

Jesus told a story about baking. Here, a woman makes bread.

dove

raven

Jesus told a story about a seed that grows into a tree. Here is a tree filled with the kinds of birds that he would have seen in Palestine.

kneading the dough

letting the dough rise

shaping flat loaves

cooking the loaves on a hot oven

hoopoe

sparrows

15 Jesus' Story About the Forgiving Father

'Here is another story,' said Jesus one day.

'There was once a father who had two sons. The elder one worked hard on the farm. The younger one wanted to have more fun.

'"I want to take my share of the family money – and go!" he said. His father was sad as he watched him leave.

'The son went to a city far away. "I'll have nice things and give parties," he laughed. It was great. Then his money ran out. He had to find a job. He ended up looking after pigs. He was so hungry he wanted to eat their food.

'"I'm going home," he said to himself. "I'd be better off as a servant on my father's farm."

'So he went. His father saw him coming and ran to meet him. He gave a party.

'The elder son was cross. "He doesn't deserve it," he said.

'"We must be glad," said their father. "It's as if he had died and come to life again."'

 In Jesus' story, one of the sons ended up looking after pigs. Jesus' people, the Jews, thought pigs were unclean. Looking after pigs was the worst job a Jewish son could imagine.

In Jesus' story, one son stayed on the farm. Here are some of the jobs he might have done.

beating olives from the tree

ploughing

sowing

hoeing flax

reaping barley

threshing

winnowing

picking grapes

looking after cattle

16 Jesus' Story About Neighbours

The religious leaders of Jesus' day grew worried. The things Jesus said did not always seem to fit with the laws they had learned.

'Which is the greatest law God gave us in our scriptures?' one asked Jesus.

'Love God with all your heart, and your neighbour as yourself,' Jesus replied.

'But how do we know who our neighbour is?' he asked. Jesus told this story:

'A man was travelling from Jerusalem to Jericho. On the way he was attacked by robbers. They left him lying in the road.

Then along came a priest. He was alarmed and hurried by. Next came a Levite. He stopped to look, then walked away. At last another traveller came, a Samaritan – an outsider. But he stopped. He bandaged the man's wounds and took him to an inn and paid for his care.

'Who was that traveller's neighbour?' Jesus asked.

'The one who helped him,' said the man.

 A priest, a man who led the worship of God in the Temple.

 A Levite, a man who helped in the Temple.

 A Samaritan. Jews and Samaritans were enemies. They had different traditions for worshipping God.

The setting of Jesus' story was the rocky road between Jerusalem and Jericho. In the hills there were many caves where bandits could hide.

17 Jesus the Teacher

Sometimes Jesus told people about God without telling a story. 'God is loving,' he said, 'and God has made the sun and the rain for everyone. In the same way, if you want to live God's way, you must love everyone – not just your friends but also your enemies.

'Don't do good things just to show off,' he warned. '*God* sees the loving things you do in secret. Your goodness will still be like a light shining in the darkness, and people will thank God for you.

'If you live like that,' he said, 'you don't have to worry about the food and drink and clothes you need. Just as God looks after birds and flowers, God will look after you.'

 In Jesus' day, some religious men used to say their prayers standing in the street so everyone would see them and admire them.

 Jesus warned that some people do good things for the wrong reasons – like being noticed.

poppy

hawk's-beard

clover

Wild flowers of the hillsides where Jesus lived. Jesus said that God makes flowers very lovely, even though they only last a day. Imagine how much God cares for people!

Jesus and the Children

One day, Jesus' friends asked him, 'Who is the greatest in God's kingdom?'

Jesus pointed to a child. 'Unless you become like children,' he said, 'you can't get into God's kingdom. When you welcome any child, you're welcoming me.'

In Jesus' day, children were not very important till they grew up enough to help their parents and work to earn money for the family. Here, children are doing everyday jobs.

Jesus welcomed children. He said that children are very important to God.

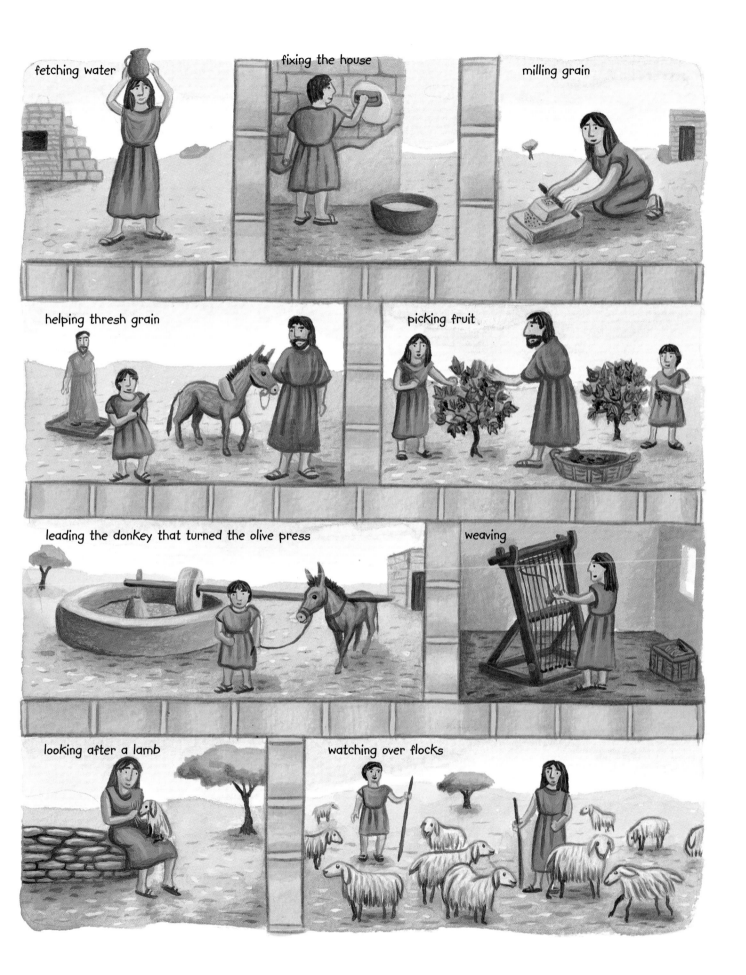

fetching water

fixing the house

milling grain

helping thresh grain

picking fruit

leading the donkey that turned the olive press

weaving

looking after a lamb

watching over flocks

Who is Jesus?

Wherever Jesus went, people gathered to see him for all kinds of reasons. They wanted to see if he would work a miracle. They wanted to hear the things he said about God.

One day, Jesus asked his friends, 'What are people saying about me?'

There were lots of answers. 'Some say you and your cousin John are really the same person,' they replied. 'Others say you're a prophet – someone who speaks for God, like in the stories in our scriptures.'

'Who do *you* say I am?' Jesus asked.

At first there was silence. Then Peter spoke up. 'I believe you're the one God has chosen to set us free,' he said.

A few days later, Peter, James and John went up a mountain with Jesus. They saw him changing to shining brightness and talking with Moses and Elijah, two other great prophets of God who had helped their people hundreds of years earlier.

 Jesus was a healer. Here is a happy family. The little girl was once so ill that she died, but Jesus brought her to life again.

 Jesus was a teacher and a storyteller. Here are crowds of ordinary people stopping their everyday work to come and listen to Jesus.

Jesus was special. The Jewish people were expecting a King chosen by God – called a Messiah or a Christ. Jesus' friend Peter believed that Jesus was the Messiah. Here, Peter, James and John see Jesus changing to shining brightness. They believe it is a sign of who he is.

Zaccheus was a tax collector. He worked for the Romans. Here, he gathers the money at his stall in the marketplace.

20 Jesus and Zaccheus

Among the people Jesus met was Zaccheus. When he heard that Jesus was visiting Jericho, where he lived, he wanted to see him.

Zaccheus was a tax collector. He was very rich, but no one liked him because he took more tax money from people than he should. He was a short man and he decided to watch Jesus from a tree so that he could get a better view.

Jesus looked up. He saw the little man nobody liked. 'Come down,' he said, 'I want to come to your house.'

Zaccheus was so happy Jesus wanted to know him! After he had spent time with Jesus, he was a changed man. He gave back all the money he had taken from people unfairly, and more besides.

coins in the time of Jesus

Zaccheus hid in a tree. Jesus looked up and saw him.

21 Jesus and the Two Sisters

Jesus had lots of friends. Martha was one of them. So was her sister, Mary.

But the two sisters were very different. Mary liked listening to Jesus. Martha couldn't forget all the housework that needed doing. When she saw Mary sitting at Jesus' feet, Martha was cross. 'Why can't Mary help me?' she asked Jesus.

But Jesus took Mary's side. 'Mary has chosen to listen to me,' he said. 'She has made the right choice.'

 Martha worked in the house. Here are some of the jobs that kept her busy.

washing

chopping

cooking

baking

tidying

cleaning

Mary listened to Jesus. He was happy to talk to her. Most teachers at that time wouldn't teach women.

Describing Jesus

Jesus used different clues to help people understand him.

'I'm bread,' he said. 'If you come to me, you won't be hungry any more.'

'I'm light,' Jesus said. 'If you follow me, you won't walk in the dark.'

'I'm the good shepherd,' he told people. 'If my sheep are in danger, I'll give my life for them.'

'I'm life,' he told Martha when her brother Lazarus died. 'If you believe in me, even when you die you'll live for ever.' And he called Lazarus back to life.

 Here is a basket of bread. Jesus said to his followers, 'I am the bread of life.'

 Here, an oil lamp brightens the darkness. Jesus said he was a light to his friends.

Here, a shepherd finds a lost sheep. Jesus said he was a shepherd to people who followed him.

A man was raised to life!
Here, Lazarus walks from
his tomb. Jesus brought him
back from the dead.

23 Jesus: The Welcome

For three years, Jesus travelled round Palestine with his friends. He told people about God and God's kingdom. He showed them how to live as God wants. At last he came into the city of Jerusalem. He was riding a donkey as a sign to show that he came in peace.

Crowds were coming to Jerusalem to celebrate the Passover festival. They saw Jesus and knew something special was going to happen. Many cheered. Some waved palm branches. Others threw their coats down to make a carpet for the donkey.

But not everyone wanted to be Jesus' friend. Some religious leaders didn't like him. 'He doesn't follow all the rules about how to behave,' they said, 'and he makes friends with people who are even worse!'

Others were afraid he would make the Jewish people fight against their Roman rulers and lots of people would get hurt or killed.

Jesus knew he had enemies. 'There is trouble ahead,' he warned his friends, but they didn't understand.

Here, Jesus rides a donkey into Jerusalem. Beyond the walls is the Temple.

Jesus in the Temple

Jesus went to the Temple. It was a place to talk and listen to God. But what did Jesus find? People were buying and selling animals to give to God. People were changing ordinary money into expensive Temple coins. It was very noisy, and people were thinking more about making themselves rich than about God.

Jesus was furious. He knocked over the tables and coins and doves flew everywhere. 'You've made God's house into a robbers' den!' he shouted.

 Here, people are trading in the Temple. It was an old Jewish tradition to offer animals and birds to God. The offering was called a sacrifice – people gave something valuable to show that God was worth even more to them.

Jesus threw the traders
out of the Temple.

25 The Last Meal

Jesus was in Jerusalem for the Passover Festival. He and his friends gathered to eat a special Passover meal. Before they ate, Jesus went from one friend to another, as a servant would, washing their feet clean from the sweat and dirt of the day.

'Just as I'm looking after you,' he said, 'so you should look after each other.'

At the meal they remembered the story of their people escaping from slavery long ago. But Jesus looked forward as well as back. He wanted this meal to be one that would help his friends to remember him when he was no longer with them.

So, when they shared bread, Jesus thanked God, broke it into pieces and told them, 'This is my body.'

When they drank wine, Jesus thanked God and told them, 'This is my blood which is poured out for many.'

As they ate, Judas, one of his friends, went out. Jesus noticed. He knew that Judas planned to tell his enemies where to find him.

 In hot and dusty Palestine it was always a servant's job to wash the feet of guests before a meal. Here, Jesus washes the feet of his friends.

Jesus noticed when Judas left the festival meal... he knew Judas was planning to let him down.

26 Jesus Alone

Judas went and told the religious leaders where to find Jesus. When the soldiers arrived at the garden called Gethsemane, all Jesus' other friends were so afraid they ran away.

Jesus was taken to the High Priest. 'Tell me more about your teaching,' he demanded.

'I've said everything openly,' Jesus replied.

'There is no more to say.'

The High Priest and the other leaders had already made up their minds that Jesus was dangerous. They went to Pontius Pilate, the Roman ruler. 'This Jesus wants to be a king,' they said. 'That's a threat to you and the Romans. You must put him to death.'

Pilate didn't think Jesus deserved to die, but

Jesus praying in the garden of Gethsemane

soldiers coming to take him

the high priest accusing Jesus

the Roman governor is asked to punish Jesus

Jesus' enemies had got a crowd together
outside. 'Kill him, crucify him!' they shouted.
Pilate feared a riot. He gave the order for
Jesus to be crucified.

Only a few of his friends and his mother
were with Jesus as he died on the cross.
Here, Jesus' mother and his friend John
are standing by the cross.

27 In the Garden

A rich man named Joseph saw Jesus die. He was a follower of Jesus, and he did what he could. 'Please let me take Jesus' body,' he asked Pilate. 'I'll have it buried.'

He and his helpers had to work fast. It was Friday and they had to bury the body before the Saturday when Jewish traditions forbade them to do any work. They pushed a heavy rock over the entrance to the tomb where his body lay.

Early on the Sunday morning, Mary from Magdala came back with some other women to say goodbye to their friend. 'Who will roll away the rock so I can get in?' she wondered.

But the tomb was open, and there was no body inside. The women told Peter and John, but they didn't believe them till they saw for themselves.

Mary stayed by the tomb. She was very upset. 'Who has taken Jesus' body?' she asked the gardener she saw standing near the tomb. The man turned. It was Jesus! He wasn't dead any more!

Jewish people wrapped the bodies of their dead in linen cloth and spices, including myrrh. Then they left the body on a shelf inside the tomb cave and slid a huge rock across the opening to close it up.

The women came to the cave.

They looked for the body.

Mary saw someone and asked where Jesus was.

28 The News Spreads

Jesus' friends heard what happened. Could they really believe such a story?

Two of them decided to leave Jerusalem and go to a village called Emmaus. As they walked, they met a stranger on the road and he started talking to them. 'We thought Jesus would bring God's kingdom to us,' they told him sadly, 'but he was put to death.'

'Our scriptures talk about how God's chosen one had to suffer,' replied the stranger. 'If Jesus was the chosen one, it had to happen that way.'

Soon they reached Emmaus. The travellers invited the stranger in for supper. He broke the bread to start the meal and gave thanks to God. As he did so, they gasped: the stranger was Jesus!

Jesus was seen by other friends of his. But after a few weeks he appeared to them for the last time and said goodbye before he went back to heaven. He told them to wait for God's help in Jerusalem. Ten days later at the festival of Pentecost, all his friends heard a rushing wind and saw dancing flames in the room. They believed this was God's Spirit coming to them to help them tell everyone about Jesus.

Ever since, Jesus' friends say they have discovered who he is by talking to each other, by thinking about his story, and by sharing bread and wine. And they say God's Spirit helps them to live life God's way.

Here, two travellers recognize Jesus as he breaks bread for the meal.

Jesus' friend Peter believed that God's Spirit gave him the courage to go on spreading Jesus' message. Here, he is talking to a crowd of people in Jerusalem. The message spread to all the world.

Important Words

angel   A messenger from God. In the Bible angels look like people but are bright and shining.

baptize   A sign of making a new start with God. The person who is baptized is dipped in water and lifted up again.

Bethlehem   A little town in Palestine quite close to the city of Jerusalem. King David, one of the greatest kings in the history of Jesus' people, was born in Bethlehem. So was Jesus.

carpenter   Someone who works with wood. Jesus probably learned how to be a carpenter.

Christ   A word from the Greek language which means the same as Messiah.

colonnade   A row of columns supporting a roof.

crucify   To kill someone by nailing them to an upright cross made of wood. Only the Romans used this way of killing people.

devil   The spirit of evil.

Egypt   A country near Palestine.

Emmaus   A village about 11 kilometres from the city of Jerusalem.

festival   A time of celebration.

fisherman   Someone who catches fish for a living. Some of Jesus' special friends were fishermen.

forgive   To be friends again with someone after they have made a mistake or done a wrong thing.

frankincense   Priests burned incense in the temple to make sweet-smelling smoke.

Galilee   The northern part of Palestine. It had a big lake, Lake Galilee, where lots of fishermen worked.

Gethsemane   A garden where Jesus and his friends met the night before he died.

God   Jesus' people, the Jews, believed God was the creator of the world.

gold   A precious metal and a gift for a king.

Herod   A Jewish king who ruled on behalf of the Romans.

High Priest   The most important priest who had special duties in the Temple and in the life of the Jewish people.

Jericho   A large town in Palestine.

Jerusalem   The most important city of the land of Jesus.

Jews   The people whose ancestors God rescued from Egypt (*see* Passover). Jesus was a Jew.

Jordan   A river that runs through Palestine.

Judas (Iscariot)   One of Jesus' special friends, but he let Jesus down and told his enemies where to find him.

laws   Rules about what to do. The Jews believe that God gave them laws about what was right and wrong and how to live (such as the Ten Commandments).

Levite   A man who helped the priests in the Temple in Jerusalem.

manger   A feeding trough for animals.

Messiah A word from the Hebrew language. It is the name for a special king sent from God. Jesus' people, the Jews, were expecting a Messiah to come and save them.

miracle An amazing event. Something out of the ordinary which points people to God.

myrrh A spice used when wrapping a dead body for burial.

Nazareth A town in Galilee. Jesus grew up in this town.

Palestine A name for the land where Jesus lived.

Passover A special festival when the Jewish people celebrated leaving Egypt hundreds of years before the time of Jesus. They were set free by God from being slaves there.

Peter One of Jesus' special friends. His name was Simon, but Jesus nicknamed him Peter, the rock. He was a fisherman.

pilgrims People who travelled to the Temple for festivals.

Pontius Pilate The Roman who ruled Palestine. Only he could give the order for Jesus to be crucified.

prayer Talking and listening to God.

priest Someone who helped people be friends with God. Priests were in charge of what happened at the Temple.

rabbi A religious teacher.

Romans The nation that ruled Palestine and many other countries in Jesus' time.

Sabbath A holy day for the Jews every week. They would not do any work on this day.

sacrifice Offering animals and grain to God to say thank you or sorry.

Samaritan Someone from Samaria. This area was between Galilee and Jerusalem. Jews and Samaritans didn't like each other because they worshipped God in different ways.

scriptures Special writings teaching people about God.

shepherd Someone who looks after sheep.

Simon *see* Peter.

sin Something wrong done on purpose.

synagogue A place where Jews prayed together and read the scriptures.

Temple This was the most important place to worship God. It was in Jerusalem.

tomb A place where a dead body was kept, usually in a cave.

wise men They were people who learned that a new king was born from studying the stars. They travelled a long way to see Jesus.

worship Gathering together to pray to God and give thanks to him.